ONE DAY AT A MOMENT.

A PRACTICAL GUIDE TO BE PRESENT IN THE MOMENT.

YUSRA LAIQ

Contents

Preface

For those who read regularly, it becomes impossible to go a day without it. Reading is a habit one loves to inculcate in their daily life. Thinking from this perspective, this book has been written to make this reading experience joyful. One day at a moment is a book which will give all the positive aspects of being present in the moment. It also provides practical guidance on how to be present and enjoy each moment of your life peacefully.

Acknowledgements

After the Almighty God, I would like to thank my parents, **Mr. Laiq Ahmad** and **Mrs. Tanzeem Laiq** who has always been a constant supporter in all the endevours of my life, and of course while writing this book, they have always encouraged me to bring positive vibes which totally reflects upon the words that I have used throughout writing this book. There is always a best source of motivation in our lives who not only tells you what is right but also supports with real guidance when things does not turns out to be right. My special thanks goes to **Ms. Saba Ubaid** and **Mr. Vivek Singh**- my mentors, for always being there and providing me with the ideas while writing this book. It would have just been a dream to achieve this milestone without their support and guidance.

Acknowledgements

CHAPTER ONE

Introduction

A book that can help you connect your academic world with the professional world.

A perfect handbook for those standing at the junction of changing their official status from a student to an employee of a company.

We all need to live each moment until we reach our ultimate destination, so why not take one day at a time and live it fully.

One day at a moment is the encouragement from my side to convince people to live in the moment. We deal with many emotions throughout our entire life, let alone talk about the life within a day with each hour passing by we are bathed with lots of different situations and experience different emotional outcomes for them, some emotions we love the most and others once gone we wish not to feel them again anytime next in future. And there are times too when we have everything, we are doing everything we want to and there's nothing we should be complaining about yet we don't feel how we want to feel. For some, that moment might be transient but for many, they last forever or may lead to the effects that cascade to the other which when compounded for a longer term affects our daily regime.

This work is greatly inspired by the quote by Thomas Carlyle:

"Our main business is not to see what lies dimly at a distance, but to do what lies clearly at hand."

We all can contribute something to our surroundings, whether within the realms of our profession or outside it. Even kind words to the person who is going through the darkest phase of their lives can be our contribution. Our duty is just to ensure that it is the positive one.

We all have 24 hours a day, we can either fill them up with our passion or just live it as it is watching movies unintentionally and complaining about our methods and efforts not working.

This book is all about managing our days. We all desire a beautiful life but we forget that life is made up of decades, decades of years, years of months, months of weeks, weeks of days, days of hours, and hours of the moment and in that moment we live. The moment you are reading this line. The moment you are breathing. This moment is the reality we often forget to live in. Nowadays, it is becoming so difficult to be present at the moment. Either we try to live in the future which often is so beautiful witihn our imaginations or in the past when something bad happened to us. No matter how short the moment was, we sometimes get stuck in it and it becomes harder to unstick ourselves with them. The more we try to get outside, the more trapped we feel and as evolution favours the survival of the fittest so we do with our thoughts- start living in that hard part of our lives, no matter how hard it is. The longer we stay in it the harder it becomes to come back and be in the moment.

To live in the moment, the most important part that's necessary is- **the realization. Realization** of the importance of the moment is what people lack nowadays. Neither do people try to live in nor do they preach the same? Needless to say how ironic it is to see in order to live peaceful and happy lives people are forcibly immersing themselves in the utter chaotic lifestyles of the world where things happen so fast that many times, it becomes difficult to even process them. Seldom do we get a moment to relax and try to understand this fact alone but the rest of the time we are always busy cursing the past. And this brings us closer to answering the question, "Why most people are unhappy nowadays?"

Normally our days are spent not living in the moment, hardly do we remember when was the last time we felt more alive.

With the advent of technology, people have become more prone to be distracted from physical work and put all their mental energy into **overthinking** even the smallest issues. This **Overthinking**, stress of work and unnecessary chaos of life is not only affecting our lifestyles but also our health where more people are prone to chronic diseases like Cardiovascular Diseases, Diabetes, High Blood pressure, Depression, Anxiety, and becoming distracted from healthy social interactions etc. Though living in the most advanced generation where technology has allowed us to get in touch with our dear ones in just a few seconds over digital devices; or get what they need in just a few seconds, people feel unsatisfied, unhappy, and distracted more than ever before.

Looking at this scenario, I have shared my insights of such moments and tried to share through means of this book why is it necessary for us to live in the moment. **Living in the moment** is so beautiful. For instance, while you are reading this line probably you are relaxed and sitting on your favourite couch or in the park or in your favourite cafe enjoying a hot cup of coffee. Just for a moment lift your head up and see how beautiful things are and there's no reason for us not to be grateful for them. And with that, I would request you to take a moment to appreciate your surroundings, be thankful for the day and focus on your role in your life, right now. Once you realize this fact your next step will always be to **mend it, improve it and live in it.** There is always one realization which makes us to live in the moment. And the moment you start living in the moment you will feel everything falling into their right places where they seem to be beautiful that even our adversities will start appearing as blessings to us.

When there's nothing bad happening outside, it is just our thoughts which make us seem we are not fine. And this is due to the fact of being not mindful of our surroundings. 70% of the time we all live in some past or in some future. It's our normal tendency to recollect every negative aspect of our lives and keep on thinking about them until a point they seem larger than they actually are. The pain we feel inside us even before the situation occurs is more effective than the actual situation. But little do we realize the fact because as usual, we all are busy collecting what bad happens with us without acknowledging what good is happening around us. Now the question comes if it's a normal process of thinking about negative situations so should we condemn it? Obviously, the answer lies in the question: it is negative, and anything negative cannot bring anything positive. The next genuine question might be the actionable step to adopt the habit of not being negative and living in the moment. Bringing this question into practical steps, I have enumerated them as follows:

Step 1: Be mindful of the surroundings.

Always be updated about what's happening around you. That not only gives you a sense of awareness but also allows you to be able to do something about it. The moment you do something or decide to solve an issue you automatically feel the moment where practically you can live in. And that is the best way to feel alive.

Step 2: Be grateful for whatever you have.

We all are busy nowadays gaining something that we consider to be lacking in our lives and this fetch in itself makes us feel that there is a need for something to fill the void. Little do we realize the fact that this void keeps on expanding with our desires. There should be a halt to this continuous quest to fill some new void every time created with the fulfilment of one desire, with a question. A question that we need to ask ourselves every now and then is: "Whether whatever we think is lacking if fulfilled would make affect our current peacefulness of mind?" If the answer is NO, then probably we are just running after something that we are unaware of how it looks like. Or the probability is that we were after some materialistic thing that will make no difference to our identity, just a badge to promote ourselves in the society. The only remedy lies in realizing whatever we have is enough for us and being grateful for that. Only then we can feel happy and live the moment which again is precious because we are living in it.

In the next few chapters, I have chunked down the whole process into actionable steps for living in the moment and how it can also be lived in a more positive and happy way.

Step 3: Always being busy will not bring the positive outcomes that we might think.

There are moments where we feel extremely sad and also situations we might be extremely grateful and happy. But this is life and we cannot remain at any extreme emotions all the time. When things fall back to normal for the rest of the time, we are neither happy nor sad we are just busy. Busy in living life which we all think will provide happiness to us. Being busy is the second nature of a person nowadays. Without planning what to do with the moment we just bury ourselves in work to fulfil some goal and when tired retire back to our beds. That's a typical life we all live. Initially, we all love living this kind of life where we need not to be mindful of what we are doing but just copying some busy schedules and then feeling satisfied with the day. But gradually as the days passed and everything seems the same we start feeling overwhelmed. **Routines** which we initially loved seem boring to us and we start looking for peace outside by binging on videos or scrolling feeds unnecessarily on our social media accounts. Little do we realize what mindless activities we are doing and what precious time we are wasting. And the fact that peace lies inside not outward gradually starts diminishing from our minds to the point that we immerse ourselves to utter chaotic lifestyles to feel peaceful. How funny and sad it is.

Being mindful of your reality always gives you a reason to be grateful for.

So, a question may arise if this is the problem then where does the solution lie? Being busy can be a choice but it's not necessary to be in that state for the rest of the time.

Living in the moment to me simply means to know what's important for now and keep focusing on that until it is completed. It can be your work or a walk in nature to unwind your thoughts and bring yourself to life again.

CHAPTER TWO

Why?

Every question that leads to a very descriptive answer begins with Why? So, I would rather prefer to question yourself why is it necessary to live in the moment? Why do we need not to be present in our dreamland always? I think preferably we all have a choice to be there but practically it will cost something which we all cannot regain back and that is our time. Why waste your efforts and time on something which will bring nothing out of it but agony? Looking from this perspective, I have given my own thoughts and pondered over this topic, and brought out every possible reason to be in the moment.

One day at a moment is a sense of realization for all of us about the truth that we all cannot live in some different times when in reality we can focus only on the moment. It's about convincing people why it's necessary to think at the moment. We all cannot feel the moment and that's why we all feel stuck for a time being and cannot move ahead. Living in the moment simply means being grateful for what we have at the moment and how it can be utilized to achieve what we desire for in the future. Sometimes in life, we start searching for ourselves externally and compare ourselves to some other personalities which we are not, but the reality is we cannot find ourselves outsides we lie inside and many a time, this comparison pulls all the negativity in our lives towards us. Little do we realize the fact the time we are born, the parents to whom we are born, the place we are born and the people we meet outside our homes are not something planned by us, which we should always be grateful for. And all these co-incidences make us unique in their own way. Instead of giving importance to this uniqueness, people have started comparing it with others. There are very few people who are away from this toxic habit and the majority of us are doing this and all thanks to the various comparing devices that we have got. Living in the moment gives us the sense of realization of who we are and what is our sole purpose to serve. One aspect of living in the moment is reminding ourselves repeatedly that we all are unique and we always have some great things to offer.

CHAPTER THREE

Success

We all are human beings and as a creature rolled in a pool of emotions we all face fears, fear could be of anything- fear of failure fear of losing something or someone, fear of not performing well when time comes, fear of being misjudged or misunderstood, fear of not reaching to our full potentials, and so on so forth, you name it. But among all, one of the major reasons for us not living in the moment is the fear of failure we experience in our lives. And this negative experience of our lives can impact our lives more negatively than we can imagine. Practically, we all cannot live a very happy and easy going lives. No matter what, irrespective of the kind of lives we are living now there comes a point where we all need to face the failure of some kind. It may be the bad results in our school years or not being able to qualify for the match that we were aiming for or failure of not being given admission in our favorite academy or the failure of rejection from your special ones, business failures or the career failures, there can be many failures to face. There are many who cannot see these failures as a stepping stone towards the success but instead considers as the mere bad luck or jinx it but many are there who does the opposite and finds this as an opportunity for improvements.

On the other hand, success has got its very own definition- "**the accomplishment of an aim or purpose**", and to attain a success we need to define our accomplishments. What we need to accomplish is what we will get in return in success and that's how we differentiate it whether we succeeded or failed. For example, if you ever had wished for public speaking and you cannot; and the fact is most of us cannot. But if you ever tried that, and still got no compliments for the talk you gave or the speech, but somehow managed to deliver your information, you will acknowledge any of the two things- Failure or success based upon the accomplishments you aimed for. If you were aiming just to speak up and stand on the stage in front of many people then it will add up to your success diary, and if you aimed for the interactions with people and standing ovations at your first go, then probably you aimed for something greater for the moment and that will create a negative experience for you. And probably in future, this will stop you from giving it another go. Imagine the other scenario, if you wished to come out of that zone and decided to go on the stage and face audience that is success. No matter how many echoes of clap you heard for that or heard a none but if you decided that this action is a success for you then probably that is Success. Many a times we held external things to be accountable for it but it's the internal achievements and barriers broken, that defines our success.

And once you define your own success instead of looking or hearing what others have to say for you or how they define it for you, even if you fail (not an actual failure but numerically) still you feel accomplished. A sense of step moving forward no matter how slow but a step forward. And at that moment you decide to go through these steps sequentially:

1. **Accept your failure as a success.**
2. **Analyze it.**
3. **Learn from it.**
4. **Optimize it if necessary.**
5. **And move forward.**

And, that is a recipe for you to learn to start living in the moment, by defining your success and learning to gain it through your own achievable steps.

CHAPTER FOUR

Optimisation

Optimization in life is really necessary for all of us to lead a healthy one. Often there are days when we struggle to wake up from bed because we think we have nothing to do and there are also days when we cannot go to bed early because we have a lot to do. Not being able to optimize our days is what brings utter chaos to our lives. We all become indecisive when it comes to answering how much we need to work per day, how much time we need to spend on each task, and how much sleep do we need keep ourselves active for the day. Sometimes we feel mentally lethargic even though we are physically relaxed, because we have used our mental energy just to decide what we need to do with the day and still towards the end of the day we feel we have done nothing just because of our multi-tasking habits, and this leads us to never stop for the day's work reminding ourselves that we have many other tasks to do. A common condition we all face and termed as **Decision Fatigue.**

The solution lies in deciding when we should stop working for the day. Distributing our tasks over the span of a week where every day is equally distributed with the main task of our projects will keep us much more relaxed throughout the week and will spare our weekends for lovely outings with our loved ones. As said by my friend Asfia,

"We all have the same amount of time, it's our choice how we utilize it."

Optimizing our time is really necessary nowadays. It simply means what discipline we have created for ourselves to complete our given projects.

From getting up from bed in the morning till the time we again get back in, there comes so many things on the way to be done by us. What we focus on is what determines how we will get our results. In order to feel content for the day, we need to prioritize our tasks. It's a logical argument that within 24 hours excluding the time we rest if we were to give at least an hour to each task still we would be able to accomplish at least 5 important tasks in a day.

Many times it so happens that our old methods do not give us the results they used to give us in the past, and hence we feel stuck in the current situations that ultimately lead to procrastination, deadlines over the head coming, late-night work and ultimately the poor quality of the work being accomplished after sometimes these outcomes bring frustrations and disappointments and all the other events that follow this regime is well known to you.

But where does the solution lies to get out of this rut? An answer to this problem lies in itself, you unwind the problem and will eventually see the solution inside it and which here I would name "Optimization". Optimization in the field of Engineering is defined as a process of the **systematic process using design constraints and criteria to allow the designer to locate the optimal solution.** If you apply the same in your daily practice to optimize the methods that you have been applying to get done with your work, you would not only be able to accomplish your task in a given time period but also would be able to feel satisfied and fulfilled with your input. That can be an easy way to feel acknowledged and feel good about your life.

Likewise, if you are a student your optimization practice would include paying attention to the subject that you are having bad grades in and ruining your overall performance. Chunk down the whole subject into it's specific different units and look for specific weaknesses and strengths in the subject and plan the next weekend ahead accordingly.

As an office employee if starting in the morning and staying up in the evening, still does not brings you closer to the results that you expect within a day, it either spills over to the next day or you have to show up till late night to show your coworkers and employees that you are a hard worker or a dedicated one when in reality you are just an exhausted soul who is fighting and finding a better way to thrive. So, the solution lies in optimizing your day. There can be questions in your mind about how this can really be possible. Before you keep on pondering the thought I would love to present a solution to this problem, and that can be followed by the steps given below:

1. **Brainstorming:** Brainstorming your daily activities and routine would be the first step to see where the problem lies. Use a digital device or a traditional pen and paper method to note them down and measure your

performance visually. This can be the hardest part but when once you decide to do that and get in the zone you will enter into the world of optimization. Things would become easier for you to take with the flow. And while doing so you would come across many activities that while performing them you wouldn't feel the difference in any of them but when you visualize them in front of you written on paper you would see what impact they can produce if eliminated, but aha "stop there" don't do it. Brainstorming them and writing them down is your priority and optimizing is in **step 3.**

2. **Checking & Eliminating:** By the virtue of your own intelligence, when you are done with the first step towards the optimizing step of brainstorming you move on to the second step and which is of checking and elimination. While doing so you need to see which activities of yours are hampering your progress. Check them out and eliminate them, from the list. Probably you would find them important for a while but here you would have to follow the **20/80 rule** which enumerates that 20% of the activities bring 80% of the important results following that you need to optimize your activities according to that 20% which are essential for your daily work and eliminate the rest, you might feel eliminating can affect your work but when you see them in the bigger picture they would probably exist but would have a little effect which would not impact as much, you might think about them.
3. **Optimization**: After breaking through the individual task that you might have been performing in a wrong way or might be putting more time and energy than required, you are ready to go adopt which are essential to maintain your productivity and which you need to work upon to bring more efficiency to the work input you are giving. Optimize the steps that you wish to adopt.

For example, every morning you start your day by looking at emails and get carried with replying to them till the afternoon, and cannot focus on the important productive work that brings most of the outcome to your performance. As another acceptable option, you need to either postpone that task to the evening or cover the midnight routine with that. The solution lies in starting your mornings with the important task first and then replying to the emails in the afternoon. There are two benefits to it:

a. People tend to reply to emails back in the late afternoon so you would not be there sitting replying to their emails back and forth as if having a real conversation.
b. If anything is important for the day itself so technically you had not lost the day and can focus on making for the important work for the day.

CHAPTER FIVE

Moment

'Being present' in the moment means to be fully engaged in the moment and making the most of it. Whether you are at a party where you are new to everyone or with your friends. Making most of the time means how you learn from people, interacting with them and learn more about the methods they adopt etc. Changing your mindset from thinking, "Oh, I seem not to belong to this place!", to "Let's see how I can interact with people and say hello to them". You will experience yourself what tremendous impact it can have upon you.

"Every occasion can be planned, but every moment has to be planned by us."

Either we can sit on the corner and complain about our previous mistakes or we can come out of our own self-made illusions and make most of it. It totally depends upon our choices and decision we make at the moment.

Now coming to the reality, many a times we all have fear of unknown, what if something goes wrong, what if that person goes away or what if that person says you are too engaging. But that's ok if you are trying to come out of your comfort zone. In the beginning all the things do not go as we all expect to be.

The solution to this problem can be, **prepare for the worst, hope for the best and expect the least.**

At the moment when you find yourself to be surrounded by the unusual condition, ask yourself: What is the best possible way to come out of this situation? What is that I can do at an individual level to solve this or Where I am limiting myself to come out of this zone?

Mindfulness is really necessary to bring this into practice. Remember that 99% problems of our lives can be solved if we just try to come out of our comfort zone and start questioning things.

Not all days are same. Some days are better than the others and some days worse as compared to rest of them. But this is life, where nothing is straightforward. Life is indeed adventurous where in order to have a smooth ride we need to focus on every crust and troughs of the journey. And thing that is always temporary is the moment we live in. Not all bad moments will last forever nor any good moments shall. So, while you are on this adventurous journey make full use of every moment. Keep what makes you happy and pull out what makes you sad. For life is too short to keep complaining about those things which are temporary.

Ask yourself what is that one activity which makes you feel happy for the day. In the beginning we will keep thinking for hours and end up with one activity that happens in a week, may be getting an extra hour nap on the weekends or maybe catching up with friend-something that is connected to externally with us will be the one thing that can make us happy. But repeatedly this exercise performed will let us know there are many things in our daily activities which makes us to live in the moment. For me it is the satisfaction I get after completing my daily writing practice or sometimes watching sunrise. And may be sometimes having deep real conversation with closed one. It can be anything which can turn out to be our stress reliever.

After getting to know about your that **"Happy Moment"**, try to inculcate in your daily routine or in the planner and enjoy it. You will gradually see that after somedays this one activity will improve your life and you will happily focus on your daily work.

CHAPTER SIX

Overthinking

"Deep thinking can build your imagination and overthink can ruin your thinking".

Although we live in the environment mentally we live inside our heads. If we say the current situation is bad we will look for every bad thing that can happen, but if we remind ourselves that the situation is a blessing even if it seems bad externally, it shall seem satisfying to us.

Overthinking nowadays is ruining the creative thinking of people, especially among the younger generation. Without any doubt, overthinking does not let us live in the moment. One of the enemies to live in the moment and enjoy the moment is this single habit of ours of not being able to prevent ourselves from overthinking. One bad outcome of overthinking can be considered is always looking at the negative side of the situation. Sometimes, so and so happens that there isn't a big issue which arises all of a sudden by overlooking the positive and entertaining the negative one. There are many things which shouldn't be given a second thought because the moment we think about them the second time we will be arising some new issues which weren't there in the first place.

Overthinking can have several forms, for instance, you are having your lunch and suddenly you start thinking about the exam you had in the morning, where your mind is not taking you towards the right answers you have written but instead makes you think about the negative outcomes of the wrong answers you might have given. Overthinking also sometimes leads us to compare ourselves with others. The most usual situation we all face in our lives is when in between a conversation with someone we think that we may sound dumb or we may be over qualified to raise any question in our minds. Remember that we all are here to learn something every day and teach something to teach every day.

We all are allowed to be students and a teacher on the same day. Not necessarily at the same moment.

Inspired by the quote, Sophia Bush

"You are allowed to be both a masterpiece and a work in progress, simultaneously"

When you start something that might not be very interesting in the beginning but as far as you go with the intention to make it beautiful it will be beautiful at the end. So, whenever thinking about something start making you feel sad, pause for a moment take a deep breath and remind yourself, this is not the moment you need to be worrying about but rather neutralizing it by your positive thoughts.

CHAPTER SEVEN

Zone

Sometimes we need to work and we procrastinate until the deadline approaches, and there are times when we just keep on thinking about the task but could not decide when to begin to work upon it. We wait for "that perfect time" to either complete it or get all the requirements for the work to get completed. Not every day is the same, sometimes we feel motivated and many times, we do not, somedays we feel confident in what we do in our lives and sometimes do not. Sometimes life happens and we lose the pace of life and that's why we feel devastated about ourselves. One thing that comes to the rescue to help us complete our work -is getting to the zone of work.

Getting in the zone of the work, here is the act of getting involved in the work so much so that you, for a time being forget about the surroundings and get to do what you need to do. For this to accomplish, you need to decide what time best works for you- mornings, evenings, late nights or whatever feels better for you- do your intense work at that time period and make a zone for that. This will help you achieve many things in your life. Some of them are:

a. **Help you complete your work.**
b. **Let you concentrate on your work.**
c. **Enhance the quality of the work.**
d. **You will form a habit which will last for days.**

The zone can be of two types:

a. Physical zone
b. Mental zone

Physical zone

Physical zones are mostly described as the type of physical place that you intend to make for your work, or more precisely your workstation. A place where you spend most of your time working. Some people might call it their workspace. Whatever you call it as make sure it is **distraction-free, a semi-comfort zone.** A semi-comfort one, so that you don't feel to fall asleep, obviously you cannot have that kind of zone in the offices but if you have a zone at your home where you spent most of your time, make sure it is comfortable enough to let you work but not very comfortable to make you sleep.

Maintaining a physical zone is very important as it offers you a better place to work and also provokes you to get back to the zone and work there, where you can actually be seen working. A good workspace can prove to be a game-changer in your performance.

Some of the ideas could be, to have your desk by the window if you have a nice view from your room, which not only help you relax your eyes but also let some natural light come in if you love to work in that.

Also, you can have some plants-artificial or real as per your preference if you like some greenery next to your working zone.

Mental Zone

Next in creating your zone of work comes the mental zone. Though different from the physical zone- which you can see or maintain according to your preference the mental zone is something which you create inside your mind. There will be some of your soft skills will come into play to maintain this kind of zone. Those soft skills include those skills that you have developed and worked upon in your life, maybe at your school or at home.

Those soft skills that will come into play are:

a. **Discipline**
b. **Habit**
c. **Routine**
d. **Punctuality**
e. **Focus**
f. **Concentration.**

Mental zone technically means what is your approach towards solving a problem and getting your work done in your own way. The mental zone is the zone where you dedicate yourself fully to the purpose you need to achieve for a few days and keep on working until it is done. In simple phrases, it can be described as how much you immerse yourself in the work until it is completed and pull yourself safely at regular intervals to remain sane. It is not necessary to remain in that zone for more days than is required. It simply means to dive deeply into the zone and keep working. There are many benefits of being in that zone. Some of them are:

a. You remain in that zone, in an amazing way even when you're not working.
b. You don't feel to procrastinate until the work is done.
c. Your work/project gets completed in lesser time than you can estimate because switching back from one zone to the other often delays the work either to the time that is met at infinity or to the deadline, in either case, the quality seems to be degraded of the output that you intend to have from the product.
d. When you are in your mental zone to complete your work, often you find solutions by yourself through the process which I term as **"incubation of the previous knowledge".** You learn how to do your work and apply the knowledge to get done, you also learn about several trouble shootings side by side which often comes into play.
e. Probably, this is something that you might think you weren't able to do before you dived into that mental zone of yours.

Making a zone often means that you pay most of your attention to that particular task until it is completed. The task can be of various forms -it can be your daily homework or a project or an upcoming exam, from anything to everything. Depending upon the task you need to complete, you will always have some time to complete it accordingly.

For example, if it is your homework then it will require a few hours if it is your project then may be possible it will require a few days and if it is your upcoming exams then maybe possible it will require a few weeks. But whatsoever the task may be, it will demand time according to its need, you have to optimize your working timetable and bring your schedule according to it, as the situation demands.

Being in the zone will help you to work according to your schedules, plans and routines. And, let you concentrate more on your work than you can do by picking some time from here and there and then completing it.

After you find your zone, your perfect time to get the productive work done, try to be in the zone as much as possible, and learn to remain in the zone, without focusing on what you don't need. That time of the day should always be dedicated to a full concentration where you don't focus on that which matters not or give you no results at all. For example, whenever you are writing something train yourself to be in that zone of writing mode and focus on what the moment demands rather than thinking about which movie you would be watching once you get done with whatever you have done and the same applies to the recreational activity if you are watching movie try to just focus on thc movie rather than thinking about some work.

There can be an experiment run to know how well you perform within your zone, both the physical and mental ones, that you have created. Start with waking up in the morning early (if you are an early bird), do your morning light routine and get started with the work which you have been postponing for weeks. Initially, you would feel resistant to even start but when you shall enter the zone, you would feel easy to go once you get started with the hardest work you have been thinking.

Benefits of creating zones:

- The emergence of new ideas when you are in the zone.
- Practice will let you enter the world in which you witness the essence of your own greatness.
- Our brain is good at providing us with the patterns once you emerge yourself in the work.

CHAPTER EIGHT

Procrastination

"Procrastinate first, Panic later"

Procrastination in literal terms is defined as the action of delaying or postponing something until it becomes very necessary to do it. What could be summarized about the procrastination in our daily life could be,

The actual reason behind your procrastination is you believe you have to do something, and many a times also knows how to do that but there is no motivation to do the work because your mind just mumbles around to know the step by step procedure to know how to accomplish something. And that's how we enter into the world of procrastination.

But as I believe there is always a solution to any problem, so the easier way to beat the procrastination can be as follows:

1. When you are doing something new, you perhaps don't have any previous neural networks formed to follow and that's why you feel excited about each step that follows. So, whenever given something, try to experiment new strategies to get your task done initially when you still have ample amount of time.
2. After you have gone through the procedure, you learn new things in a better way. This enables you to follow many mind maps or protocols to follow later. As, it is easier to forget something when you are out of the practice of any procedure.
3. Once you are in the zone do not try to get distracted, whatever the reasons you find nearby to you for the procrastination make sure you have already removed them from the place.
4. Do not try to multitask and switch between different task simultaneously.
5. Always make a habit to start working on something simple and complete easier steps first and then follow what comes by. Starting with something

hard would always land you in the trap of not doing it and ultimately in the habit of procrastination.

CHAPTER NINE

Improvements

"Opportunities ends only when we stop trying."

Each day we are presented with many choices. Choices can be of any sort, whether you get a call from your friend or you are invited for a dinner from your relative or simply just a new opportunity to expand your business and there can be 'n' number of good opportunities, you name it. Conversely, there can also be some negative situations in your lives- a call from a friend whose father has just suffered a heart attack or a relative who has just met an accident and many other things can happen. It comes to the point that we all are presented with many choices, situations and opportunities every day. Not every day is the same for all of us, now the question comes of what to focus on and what not to. Places change, circumstances change, environment change, people change, and sometimes everything changes. and, above all change has always been a law of nature, many things change altogether but what remains constant is our expectation that nothing at any point of our life will change. At that point in our lives, one thing should always remain constant and that is the desire to accomplish something. No matter where you stand in your life, whatever your conditions are take them in your stride and keep moving forward by just following the path of improvement. You don't look upon the world for what they think about you or about your work, if you are determined to achieve something just keep your eye on the destination and always try to follow the right Path-path of improvement, a path of truth, the path of honesty and path of kindness.

Improvements can only be made on something which we already created not on something which we thought of and never accomplished it. Even if we ever thought of public speaking we can only improve it if we ever tried that once no matter whether that experience was good or bad. The key to improvements is Regular practice. No matter you failed today in communicating well with your manager, there's always a second opportunity to mend it.

CHAPTER TEN

Courage

Life is a practical collection of events it is not always possible that you will get what you invest for. You will be defeated, you will be betrayed you will lose trust in people and you will be tested by the universe by every means to prove that you deserve to be at the place that you aim for. And that will be real show time where you do not need to lose the courage and have to be limitless, it is possible that you might be putting more effort than ever before, you can be struggling every bit every now and then at the end getting no results out of it and a point will come that you will start questioning your own efforts but never lose courage and also never lose belief upon yourself that do you really deserve to be at the place where you think you can be.

At that point of your life, it is possible you will feel lost, alone, shattered and worthless but that will be the point in your life where you will require your own support more than ever before. Because the moment you will lose your belief upon yourself you will remain none. It requires more than hard work to get to the place where you want to be and that is **Courage** to be yourself and focus on the path of improvement. And the moment you decide not to accept failure as part of your identity you will regain yourself as a whole and automatically your brain will start flushing with ideas to get out of the rut you have been stuck into.

It is true that when things actually happen outside of our heads we feel differently about them. Maybe sometimes we feel more attached to it or less, depending upon how we perceive them before but life happens always, and at that point of our life we need to remind ourselves that we are just human beings and we are allowed to do mistakes like others but not what goes against the humanity, we learn a lot by them. This way we can allow ourselves not to be harsh on ourselves, we can make mistakes, realize them, learn from them and move on. Sitting on your mistake and keep regretting them will be the second mistake of wasting our time. We are allowed to be always in the learning phase in our lives. Learning should never stop and that's how we keep on refreshing ourselves every day and keep improving for the sake of "better us" for tomorrow. Being not the prisoner of our own thoughts or past mistakes, we somehow allow ourselves to be a guest to our present moment and enjoy and live in the moment to the fullest.

CHAPTER ELEVEN

Tracks

Life is full of surprises, uncertainities and many other moments. To be very precise, not even a single moment is the same. Every moment is different from the other. Often in our lives, we all face something that we had never wished for, and many times these circumstances distract us from the normal regime of life. For example, we may fall sick for a longer duration, or we may have to look after someone or most, unfortunately, we may lose someone but according to rules of the nature, our lives need to move forward no matter what. It becomes hard to bring our lives back on the track. That's when the real philosophy of our lives comes into play. Changes in track also affects the focus of our life. It is possible that we plan, work upon them and execute them and things do not go as we expect them to be. We take risks in our lives hoping for the best and expecting for the worst and still worst happens and we have to go through them. At that point in life bringing ourselves to the track of life often becomes difficult. We think that life will follow the patterns that used to be followed in life and when things keep worsening and the outcomes keep on disappointing us just because we follow the past trends that once brought us results but sometimes it stopped giving us results. We keep on trying to give our best and we accomplish giving our best but the results keep on backfiring our plans.

Same at that moment, what you need to do is put a halt on all the activities that are failing methods and look upon your strategies once again and change them for a while to achieve your goals. Mostly the strategy to recheck your strategies should be to change the previous strategies to bring the best for yourself.

Sometimes we have the right amount of potential, courage and intelligence but we still cannot help ourselves to get to that level, just because of our inability to follow the right strategy. Just like the factory works if you have the right proportions of the raw material to make candy but if you cannot perform with the right strategy, every effort of yours will always seem to be doomed.

So the right strategy is the key to accomplishing what you want. It can be anything may be from life to the small projects you are working upon. And it is not necessary that the strategy that once worked for you will always work for you. It is possible you need to put some extra milestones or change a bit to get what you are working upon. And changing your strategies will always work in your favour which will help to acknowledge the present moment and live in that too.

CHAPTER TWELVE

Purpose

"The deeper our purpose of life is the more we enjoy whatever we do in our lives."

What is the purpose of this life? This is not the answer which we will perhaps be answered from within us. Every act done purposefully is what makes us stay positive and productive throughout the day. For example, in your school years if your purpose is to learn something new. Then learning something every day and applying your newly gained knowledge in the subject can become easier for you to learn your chapters easily every day and solve your exercises. On the other hand, if your purpose is just to pass the exams then probably you will open your books just a few days before the exams. Similarly, if you aim to learn to cook food you will end up being in the kitchen a few days a week but if your purpose is to help your mother then every day then you will be in the kitchen on regular basis. And here comes the role of the purpose in our lives. Our purpose in life not only gives meaning to our lives but also lets us do the needful activities at the moment.

Living in the moment is not harder when you know exactly what you should be doing at that moment. And that realization comes from the act of mindfulness of the moment. Your purpose is what tells you what you should be doing right at the moment. The deeper the meaning of your purpose the more you shall enjoy the moment and the more you will feel content with whatever you do with it.

"A vision and purpose of yours hold no meaning unless it is visible in your actions."

CHAPTER THIRTEEN

Planning

A good strategy and the plans always enables a person to accomplish something in a very satisfying manner.

Planning your day gives you much clarity to your day where you need not to be worrying about your next steps. The good thing about it is even if you accomplish 60% of the task at the need of the day you will feel accomplished for the day.

Planning your day gives you much satisfaction for you the day ahead. It gives the structure to your day, where every now and then you need not to be thinking what to be doing next. But, there's one thinks which we may do it wrong and that is being over-ambitious for the day. While planning your day don't be overambitious. Look for the most important task in your list. Plan accordingly and add them in your list.

As said by my friend, Salah

"Planning your day gives you structure what to do, lest it is like a boat sailing in the sea aimlessly."

The only limitations are the intensity of our desire to achieve it. Once we believe in it, the next step is to convert them in actionable goals and chunking them down in actionable steps.

Breaking down the task into small actionable steps often helps one to motivate and accomplish the task easily and that too in a very less time. For example, just think about the important presentation you need to give next month over the reports that you have gained so for any project you are currently working upon. The moment you think about it and you feel anxious and nervous how you are going to do that and secondly the fear may also arise if you aren't able to present the data properly in front of your boss. The fear comes in its own packages having their own significance individually. Sounds familiar right, now what comes into rescue is **planning, planning and planning**. A good planning not only helps you feel relaxed and focused on one task at a time but also helps you to maintain your productivity throughout the process.

A good planning involves a strategy to solve any task and get completed before the deadline.

A rough draft for the presentation preparation can be given be as follows:

Task Name

Deadlines

Remarks

STEP 1:

STEP 2:

STEP 3:

STEP 4:

STEP 5:

FINAL PREPARATION:

CHAPTER FOURTEEN

Platforms & Roles

We as an individual has many duties to perform at a time on different stages of our lives. And which duty to apply when is determined by the place we stand for the moment.

For instance,

- If we are in school/ University for having education, we are demanded to focus on our studies and be a good student. If we are at the same place standing as a knowledge worker, then our duty changes and focus demands to behave as a responsible education provider.
- Likewise, being with people in the same working zone we are allowed to be who we are complain about our daily life, talking about that "always complaining boss" or discussing about the new policies introduced in the society.
- At home we are someone's child, someone's parent, someone's siblings and we have to react accordingly.
- While commuting to our work place we are just passenger observing our surroundings, people's reaction and sometimes just focusing on our journeys.
- In the supermarket we are customers who need to buy essentials to accomplish our duties of home.

So, in a way we can say we are not a single individual we are collection of different roles in a single person and that explains a lot. Now ask yourself when you decided to be best player of your role. When you avoided that argument just you were frustrated for your academics with your family. When was the last time you let go off your sibling take of our favorite perfume without your permission? You could have been a person who loses temper very easily if someone else must have done that but acknowledging the place you were present and the role you had to play at that moment you decided to be in the role for a while.

Our places decide the role we need to play at that moment. And for our realization we have to be mindful of our activities that what we are doing and what's the demand of the situation.

Here a very limiting role is also played by the technology we are surrounded nowadays. The question is why we cannot realize our roles in our life at the moment as this simple fact is just because we are more focused on competing with the technology not with people but what people are putting on online. And that's all what makes the matters worst even without our realization.

Accepting the fact that technology and relations have very specific and different roles in our lives can be best rescue to get out of this zone and be present as our roles in life demands.

CHAPTER FIFTEEN

Start

"Start with small actionable steps."

Starting with what you love to do is the harder part for any work. I will discuss what is the hardest part later on, but here I am mentioning what are the key strategies to start with what you need to achieve. Fresh starts are always beautiful, you are hyped with new energies and you have many ideal plans of what you believe you are capable of. But believing and achieving lies in two different spectra if you are unable to meet them both with your intellect power.

And the first step to achieve what you believe you can do is **Strategic planning**.

If you are able to plan what you want, then you are half way through it. Because often when we start doing something we always get carried away with what we started and are unable to take a break andreflect upon and start again with new start line that will demand both cost time and energy. The most practical approach could be a better planning for what you want.

Yes, if something goes wrong then we can optimize it pausing for a moment but never we can plan in between. So a better planning strategy works best if you are working what you want in life. There can be few steps to start what you need. They are:

Start with an ambition and vision

The first step towards starting something is- with whatever you want to plan for have an ambition and vision for that. If you don't have the end goal then all you will be doing is releasing arrows all around without any directions, no matter how good you are at that skills but all you would be doing is releasing them aimlessly which perhaps at certain point will become futile and questionable.

So having an ambition that you will complete what you are staying is the foremost important thing before you start something to do and the vison should also be clear before you start something because having an end goal you will end up somewhere but that place will be unrecognizable to you.

Start with small amount of efforts in the beginning.

After having the strategic planning, all you need to be able to work upon the plan in actionable steps. Having an actionable step will enable you to have more practical approach towards your vision. Thinking that you would achieve the next competitive exam could be your vision or building a company of yours could be the vision, but if you are unable to figure your next step, you would never achieve what you need in your life. For example, if what you aim to achieve is a long term goal that lies in 5 years. Your next step should be to have yearly plan which further broken into the monthly plan and monthly into weekly and weekly into tomorrow's to do list.

So, a strategic planning and having a vision both should show cooperativity if you aim to achieve with what you have started.

CHAPTER SIXTEEN

Stop

Starting something is always an easy task. In the beginning we all posses new energies, new plans, and new visions to get along with that but as the time passes the energy that we initially had, gradually diminishes and all we face is burnout conditions, procrastinations, sometimes overwhelmed with the workload and many a time there is seen no progress at all. These all lead to mere disappointment and many times it so may happen that we are unable to figure out which way to move forward or when is the time to stop and consider our work to be accomplished. The latter one is more dangerous as not knowing when to stop often leads to the condition of burnt-out in people, and ultimately their professional life starts to affect their personal lives as well. For instance, they are unable to focus on the present moment, they seem to be always mentally present in their workplace and their brain always keeps processing to figure out the next result to achievement to be made in their current project, and they might keep on struggling to get rid of that situation which later affects their mental health, their relationship with their families and friends. Have you ever seen a person sitting at the corner at the most happening party, not at all involved at the moment? The same person who used to never miss a second to enjoy the parties, that is what we consider as the burnt-out conditions.

You might have also witnessed the condition where you are unable to focus on one task at a time, and keep on switching from one task to another, which is often considered a waste of time because as soon as you start to focus on one task you try to figure out how to steer your way through it you seem to switch to the other one which again initiates for the beginning and you seem to have brain drainage condition. Because this habit does not help you get anywhere with your work but still is an energy-consuming strategy.

Getting carried away with the work and not knowing when to stop has its own disadvantages which not only adversely affect your work but also deteriorate a person's health specifically targeting their mental health. There can be many strategies to avoid this to happen to oneself, but the foremost lies in mending some of the daily habits. Adopting some healthy habits after starting some great project or work can get us far in our career and also have a healthy relationship with ourselves.

Some of the strategies are:

1. **When you design your work know when to stop, and also when to take breaks without affecting the flow of work:** There's always a process to initiate something and when you initiate something the first step is always to plan ahead. Planning ahead has benefits of its own where you can focus on the task on one hand and then move to the other.
2. **Set a timer for every task on a daily, weekly and monthly basis: After setting a timer, make yourself, a to-do list mentioning your end goals not how you will start the task.**
3. **When you find yourself switching between two or more tasks leave everything for a while and relax.**
4. **Focus while doing your work:** The key to accomplishing something for the day is to maintain focus for long hours throughout the day. Whether it be any task which you love to do, it is your responsibility of yours to accomplish., if you cannot maintain focus for long hours you would not enjoy to do your work. So, in short in order to enjoy your day you need to maintain your focus for the work or vice versa.

Now the question may arise how can one achieve that focus? And the answer is simple, find something you love to do. That requires a lots of research upon yourself. You need to find which is that one task of your day for which you can wait or that in which you lose the track of time while doing so.

Certainly on the other hand it doesn't mean you need to stick around your desk for the whole day, but something in which you can engage yourself for hours effortlessly.

There's no dragging force involved in your work when you need to do what you love to do. We all love to do different things, and that one thing most alive to live in the moment. What lies in future or what holds in our past is just a matter to be considered for no concern for us. That is the beauty of doing our work. When the time passes you never know.

CHAPTER SEVENTEEN

Time Management

There are many ways you can manage your time to match your commitments. But before we dive into how to do that, I would rather prefer to discuss what actually time management is. As the next steps follow this one, how do you define time management? Let me tell you what time management exactly means- what you decide to do with the time you have when you are on your own. At any hour of the day, you do exactly what you mean to be doing with that hour. So, based upon that analogy it's wise enough to plan your day ahead so that you can prioritise your important activities at the most productive hours of the day. This strategy will help you maintain your focus on one task at a time and you will not keep worrying about what to do next, this will also not leave extra free time where you keep procrastinating. Time management also means you gain control of your free hours and can utilize those hours in resting for a while.

A simple guide to managing your time could be in such a way.

1. You can make your day's rough draft based on the activities you spent your hours on.
2. A simple diagrammatic representation can be as follows:

Sleep-7 hours
Office/School- 7 hours
Commute-1 hour
Lunch/Dinner/Breakfast- 3 hours
Self-care/Bath-2 hours

Based upon this rough draft you get **4 hours extra** on a typical work day to spend on your leisure activities which can include spending time with your family, your windup work, going out on a nature walk or just spending an extra hour to plan your next upcoming project. You decide it.

In this way roughly calculating your day can give you access to your day where you can unleash your potential for some productive work.

CHAPTER EIGHTEEN

Disconnect

The literal meaning of disconnecting is- cutting off from something. That is actually what I would focus on in this section. Often it is necessary to vibe with your own self and listen to your own voices. There is always something disturbing going on in the outer world. The things are not in order, there are plenty of emails to be answered, you need to pay bills, the monthly report is due next week, vendors are delaying your orders, your supervisor is on leave and you need important papers to be forwarded by him/her, your bills for the project has not been cleared and many more adds on the list, you name it. Tackling them all often becomes overwhelming. Waking up in the morning, going through morning routine and again getting ready for the new battle to face. The same tasks done repetitively becomes overwhelming and again and again you become tired by those everyday situations. There comes a point where it seems pointless to wake up every day in the miserable condition and facing the messier world. The only solution lies in distracting or disconnecting yourself from the world for every now and then. This totally reflects upon your performance and work productivity.

So, a question might come if distracting from the world is so much necessary, then what could be the actionable steps to do that. There could be many but here I have summarized them in few steps which can be easier to follow if you are willing to follow them. They are:

a. **Utilize your weekends to spend time with yourself.**
b. **Spend time with yourself maybe outside in natures & vibe with yourself.**
c. **Read Books**
d. **Start practicing meditation.**
e. **Increase your focus on prayers.**

f. **Have a deep meaning conversation with your very closed ones.**
g. **Start journaling and writing about how you feel every now and then.**

Above mentioned steps could be an actionable guide to distract yourself from the world for a while. Disconnecting yourself from the outer world does not mean you disconnect yourself fully and just be on your own all the time. It means to be disconnect yourself from the outer world's chaos and connect with the inner world where you perhaps live all the time.

The above mentioned steps has their own benefits which are explained below:

a. **Utilize your weekends**: When the schedule is automatically updated with hectic works from Monday to Friday, your mind automatically starts craving for Saturdays. There can be a reason you may plan for parties, obviously social gatherings are important but what if you plan to reconnect with yourself and spent time with your own self, there can be no other better way to do that or the better way could be to have some recreational activity at that hour of the day.
b. **Spend time with yourself:** Now, there can be a void if you decide to utilize the weekend to disconnect from the world to what to do with that day/ hour. In order to fill that void a better way could be go out for walk in nature, read your favorite genre book, have a brief overview of the week and track where you spent most of the hour, ask yourself can that hours be optimize to get most productive work in lesser time, write journals address how you felt for that weekend, put your mobile phone or all the other digital devices aside, which might disturb you, go out and spent time with your friend and have some deep conversations. Sometimes, it so happens that your close friend can bring those points clearer to you about yourself which perhaps might not be clearer to you as before.
c. **Focus on Meditation:** If you are a spiritual person, you can also go on for practicing regular meditation. Meditation can help you reconnect with your body and get outside of your head. Many a times it so happens our fears, weaknesses, shortcomings and insecurities are if left unaddressed for longer term they start turning into anxiety, depression, undecidedness, and many other negativities, which perhaps harms our mental health and affects our productivity. We all are human beings and

we all have some strengths and weaknesses. If we keep on relying on our strengths to bring the desired outcomes, unintentially we start ignoring the weaknesses, which also needs to be addressed at regular intervals and with the troubleshootings. Meditations often helps us to focus on our body and regains the lost mental positive energy which we require to go along with strengths we have.

There can be many other ways that you can utilize to disconnect yourself from the outer chaotic world and reconnect yourself with the inner peaceful world. Based upon the above mentioned steps you can also form your own ways to disconnect, but make sure whatever links you with external world you put that aside just for a while and then see the magic of your inner self that would bring peace to you.

CHAPTER NINETEEN

Process

Accomplishing something or reaching some point requires you to go through the process. A process that includes steps and turns. Mind you, process is simple but not easy. For example, becoming a surgeon can be your goal and achieving your goal requires you to go through the process, that process could be passing your high school exams, then studying for medicine would require you to get admission to a good medical school which is itself a subset of processes, after getting admission there are terms and exams you need to pass and then your final internship session on which whole of your career depends and then you choose your field to specialize and ultimately again get internships as a resident and then there are other processes for promotions through which you enter into the profession of being an actual surgeon. Now, taking from here I would like to explain the process of becoming a surgeon could be a simple process when you know the step-by-step procedure but not an easy one. Going through the process in itself is a very complicated process where you need to face all the practical things which perhaps you would never add to your wish list to face.

Achieving something always requires you to go through the process and it is the process that decides where you stand. There are many things that come into play while going through the process and tackling them all with sincerity decides where we stand in the field. Okay, from here I will take the explanation. Every goal or dream of yours will have a certain process and that process is not composed of just hard work, dedication, sincerity towards the people you are working with, honesty and all the positive adjective you can define to do what it requires but also contains various other strategies that perhaps we may define as negativities of life.

Combining them all they become a part of the process. No matter what kind of input or how improved and refined your methods are, still you will have to go through these steps because going through these 5 steps will reveal truly who you are as a person and why you deserve the title or purpose you are working for.

Oftentimes, achieving what you want you will come across these things and where you might not be getting the results as you expected or as you hoped for before investing your positive and honest efforts in what you want and suddenly all the things start changing abruptly that you start questioning your own efforts, at this step your real principles come into play that will perhaps help you keep moving forward.

Remember that once, you are in the process, build the habit of not leaving the process before you accomplish what you want from your life. No doubt these five adversities will come into the picture but they are blessings in disguise for the person that deserves the purpose that you are working for and also brings the best version of yours that is in itself a unique way of building yourself.

Yes, it is possible that time and again we will start feeling exhausted after investing energy again in the same process and not being able to get what we expected, then as a human being you are allowed to take rest whenever you feel or when you find is the most appropriate way you should take the rest and then resume with the battle of accomplishing what you want.

Whenever you decide to take a break and focus on what you want by having a little relaxation time, it's better to plan your break. Initially, you will not be able to predict how many hours each task or strategy would take but once you are able to adjust to that it is better to plan your break strategically so that you are able to work efficiently without breaking the flow of your work and also the quality of your work is not degraded at all.

Remember, the process is not easy, so do not lose focus while you are in the one. Losing your focus will cost you no the accomplishment of your work because either taking breaks at an unappropriated time or not focusing on what you want while in the process you might lose track which perhaps does not cause you any immediate loss but when compounded on the long term can efficiently reflect upon your results and performances.

Before you dive into the subject or the task in itself, just built the habit of knowing the bigger picture, learn about the process or procedures that you shall apply later on and as soon you are able to learn what could be the best strategies to face the situation, also learn to apply immediately.

The biggest advice that you would ever hear is "never stop learning." Train your mind to always learn new things because every day there is always something to learn. To build a habit to keep learning and getting ahead in your field.

After you started learning the process and allow to tackle at every point and are in the midway, forget the habit of quitting. This habit in itself will help to get through the process efficiently and you will also learn what your shortcomings are and what kind of troubleshooting it requires, so that can get the chance to improve every day.

So here I have mentioned all the argumentative points to stress the importance of going through the process and strategies to tackle them each. These can be helpful while you are going through one.

The greatest benefit of going through any process to achieve what you want is that you learn a lot about yourself.

CHAPTER TWENTY

Be Yourself

"What you don't express is not comprehended as well."

What does "be yourself" means to you? Often we play with this adage wrongly and mess things up. For me, it's more about finding your uniqueness and improving it. Necessarily being ourselves and following our true selves we will reach the place where we need to be.

What actually does it mean, can be explained by these examples: if you feel like you are not surrounded by the right people, Be one. If you feel you are not getting attention from them, start paying to them. If you feel people are not patient enough to understand you, understand them and then explain to them what you need.

Often we accept the fact that change in society cannot be brought but we forget the fact that we are also part of that society, change can also be bought from us. We can contribute to the change in society.

If you see something's wrong, get yourself to change it. The first step toward improvement is the realization of what's wrong from your side. Once you realize the inputs from your side work upon them in your own way.

Being yourself simply means "**realizing what unique qualities do you possess and refining them with time.**" We all are born unique and surely we all have something unique to offer to people.

After some point in our lives, we would not be appreciated for what we do, and that's how we learn to be ourselves. That no matter how many positive inputs you give, you would never be appreciated or celebrated for that and at that point as a human being it is very much possible to feel disappointed but that is the moment we all need to learn and remind ourselves: "this is what I have done for my own satisfaction and this act of mine would not be appreciated whatsoever it happens." At every point, you need to remind yourself that it's ok to be not part of the appreciation team, and you connect yourself with the greater purpose that is sufficient to make you feel satisfied.

Being yourself is sometimes taken in the wrong perspective, people start to believe in the heat of the moment that it is ok to be just anyone and that spectrum of anyone covers all the negative attitudes towards others. But that does not encompass what we want or what we desire.

CHAPTER TWENTY-ONE

Routine

Routines can be defined as some tasks which we tend to repeat on a regular basis in sequential order. Now, what role does a routine play in our lives? Routines are something in which we immerse ourselves on the regular basis. Why is it necessary to have routines? First of all, those who follow them either intentionally by being self- disciplined or unintentionally by following regulations set by the organization or institutions they are working under, they might have experienced the fact that they are least likely to get distracted from what they need to do in their lives.

Routines play a major role in someone's life and specially to keep yourself on the track of life. Building a routine, not only keeps you move forward but also keeps a check on your daily activities and feel relaxed for the time you are involved in the work.

Conclusion

There can be various strategies to achieve what you want but the best one is one that you choose for yourself. Stop following the trends or walk the same path trodden by people before you. You can have your own path and explore every new and good thing that perfectly resonates with you and bring the peace that you choose to live in and the peace that chooses out of no doubt.

Combining these all, what you need to do with your life you have got your present moment which in itself a present for you live in that. So, make the best use of it, anyhow life happens with everyone but the ruling says **life keeps moving.**

There are a few quotes of mine which I love and would show through this piece of work.

"You become creative once you start falling in love with your work. And, that is the key to how you master your skills."

"At every point of your life, you would not know everything about something, at that point it will be just your level of your satisfaction which will make you move forward."

Printed by Libri Plureos GmbH in Hamburg,
Germany